Explorers!

Christopher Columbus

Famous Explorer

Arlene Bourgeois Molzahn

Enslow Publishers, Inc.

40 Industrial Road	PO Box 38
Box 398	Aldershot
Berkeley Heights, NJ 07922	Hants GU12 6BP
USA	UK

http://www.enslow.com

To my granddaughter Anna who is my greatest explorer.

Library of Congress Cataloging-in-Publication Data

Molzahn, Arlene Bourgeois.
    Christopher Columbus : famous explorer / Arlene Bourgeois Molzahn.
       p. cm. — (Explorers!)
    Summary: Discusses the life of Christopher Columbus, with an emphasis on his career as an explorer.
    Includes bibliographical references and index.
    ISBN 0-7660-2066-5
    1. Columbus, Christopher—Juvenile literature. 2. Explorers—America—Biography—Juvenile literature.
3. Explorers—Spain—Biography—Juvenile literature. 4. America—Discovery and exploration—Spanish—
Juvenile literature. [1. Columbus, Christopher. 2. Explorers. 3. America—Discovery and exploration—Spanish.]
I. Title. II. Explorers! (Enslow Publishers)
E111 .M76 2003
970.01'5'092—dc21   2002005114

Printed in the United States of America

10 9 8 7 6 5 4 3 2 1

Illustration Credits: © 1999 Artville, LLC., p. 12; Corel Corporation, pp. 17, 22, 24, 37; DigitalVision, p. 18 (map); Enslow Publishers, Inc. using © 1999 Artville, LLC. images, pp. 4 (map), 8, 15, 21, 43; Library of Congress, pp. 1, 4 (portrait), 6, 7, 10, 13, 14, 16, 18 (top), 20, 23, 26, 28, 29, 30, 31, 32, 34, 35, 36, 38, 40, 41, 42.

Cover Illustration: background, Monster Zero Media; portrait from the Library of Congress.

Please note: Compasses on the cover and in the book are from © 1999 Artville, LLC.

Contents

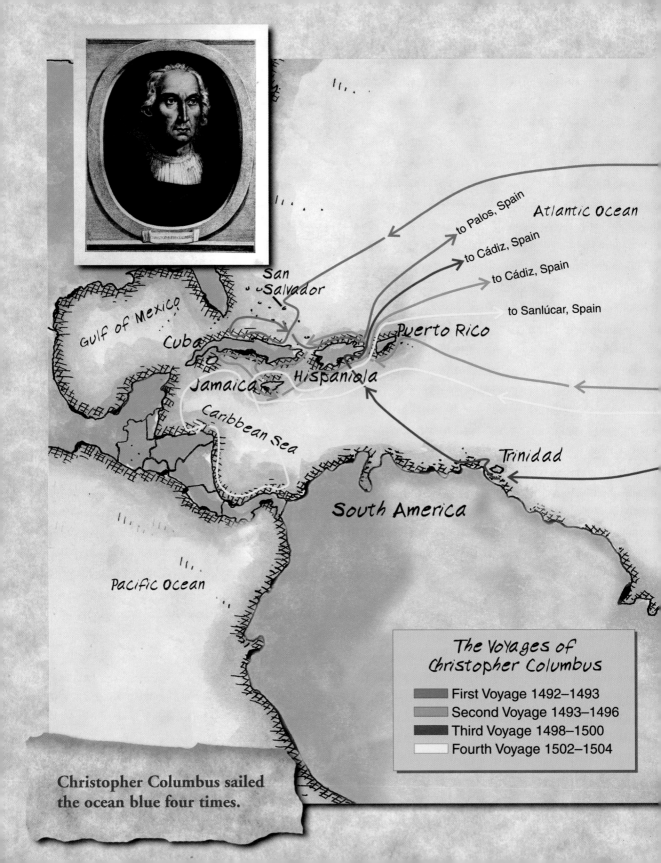

to Palos, Spain

Atlantic Ocean

to Cádiz, Spain

to Cádiz, Spain

to Sanlúcar, Spain

San Salvador

Gulf of Mexico

Cuba

Puerto Rico

Hispaniola

Jamaica

Caribbean Sea

Trinidad

South America

Pacific Ocean

The Voyages of Christopher Columbus

First Voyage 1492–1493
Second Voyage 1493–1496
Third Voyage 1498–1500
Fourth Voyage 1502–1504

Christopher Columbus sailed the ocean blue four times.

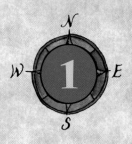

Shipwrecked

It was the morning of August 13, 1476. Twenty-five-year-old Christopher Columbus was sailing on the ship *Bechalla*. The *Bechalla* was sailing with four other ships from Genoa, Italy. They planned to make stops in countries in northern Europe.

The ships from Genoa were sailing along the coast of Portugal. They came under attack from a fleet of fifteen enemy ships. Cannons were fired. The battle lasted all day. The sailors on the five ships from Genoa fought long and hard. But they were no match for the fifteen enemy ships. After ten hours of fierce fighting, fires started on

Ships battling in the ocean might have looked like this.

some ships. Black clouds of smoke filled the air. Soon all the ships from Genoa were on fire. Many sailors died on the ships. Other sailors jumped off the burning ships and drowned.

Columbus had been shot. The bullet was still in his leg. His ship was on fire and sinking fast. Now Columbus knew there was only one thing to do.

He jumped from the burning ship. As he hit the water, he saw a long oar. He grabbed the oar and began swimming. Land seemed miles away, but he did not give up. Columbus swam six miles to shore. He landed in Lagos, Portugal. People in Lagos took care of him.

Ships looked like this during Columbus's time.

As soon as his leg healed, Columbus headed for the city of Lisbon, Portugal. He went to live with his brother, Bartholomew, a chartmaker in Lisbon. Columbus helped his brother make new charts and maps. Sailors always wanted the latest charts. New discoveries were being made about the islands in the Great Sea. Today the Great Sea is known as the Atlantic Ocean.

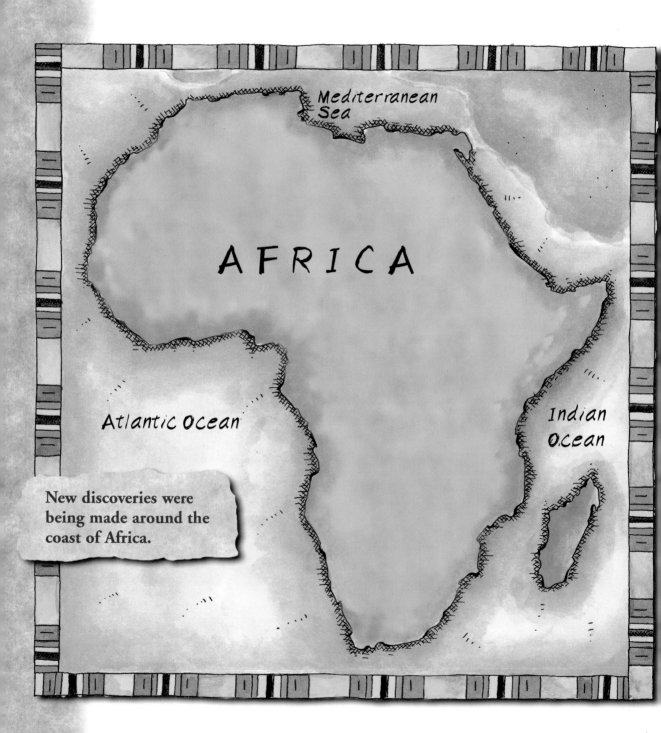

Mediterranean
Sea

AFRICA

Atlantic Ocean

Indian
Ocean

New discoveries were
being made around the
coast of Africa.

New discoveries were also being made around the African coast. As soon as a discovery was made, new charts and maps were needed. Old charts and maps had to be fixed. The brothers had a good business.

Talk of new discoveries made Columbus want to go back to sea. He wanted to sail out on the Great Sea. All the maps of that time showed the world as one large island surrounded by water.

In February 1477, Columbus left his brother's shop. He became a sailor on a ship that sailed far out into the Great Sea. Some people believe the ship went to Iceland. Others believe the ship went to Ireland. When Columbus returned that spring, he knew he wanted to sail farther on the Great Sea.

This is what one painter thought Christopher Columbus looked like as a young man. No one really knew what Columbus looked like.

The Early Years

Cristoforo Colombo was born in Genoa, Italy, in 1451. In Spanish his name is Cristóbal Colón. To many he is known as Christopher Columbus. His parents were Domenico and Susanna Columbus. Domenico was a wool weaver who made cloth.

Christopher Columbus was the oldest of five children. It is not certain if he went to a school or if he was taught at home. He must have been a good student because he learned to read and write. He also learned math, astronomy, and geometry. These are subjects that were needed to sail a ship. Being the oldest, he probably also helped his father in the weaving shop.

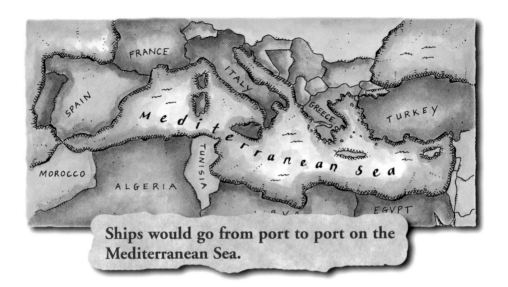

Ships would go from port to port on the Mediterranean Sea.

Columbus spent most of his free time on the docks. At this time, the city of Genoa was a great trading center. Ships brought goods to the city from Europe, Asia, and Africa. Columbus watched the sailors. Being a sailor must have seemed more exciting than being a weaver.

Columbus went to sea at a young age. He worked as a deckhand on a ship. These ships went from port to port trading goods along the coast of the Mediterranean Sea. Columbus watched and listened. He learned a lot about commanding a ship. He heard a lot of stories about the Great Sea beyond the Mediterranean.

Many people believed strange things about the Great

Sea. Some sailors told stories about giant sea monsters that lived in the Great Sea.

Columbus did not believe the stories about the giant sea monsters. Columbus believed that if he sailed west he would find a water route to the lands in the East. He believed that he would return with a rich cargo of spices and silk goods.

Columbus married Felipa Perestrello Moniz, who was from Portugal, in 1479. A year later, they had a son named Diego. The family lived in Portugal for the next five years.

Many people believed monsters lived in the sea.

Treasures of the Indies

The countries of India, China, Japan, and the East Indies were known by one name. People in Europe called the whole area the Indies. There was a route to Europe from the Indies. Goods, like spices and silk, were brought by boat on the Red Sea. Then the goods were loaded onto camels and taken to Europe. The route was dangerous.

Here is Columbus with his family.

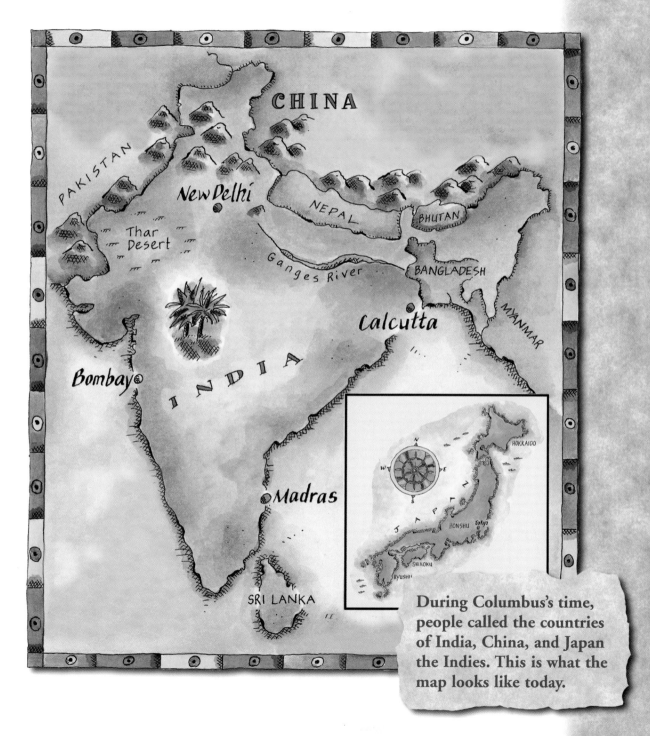

During Columbus's time, people called the countries of India, China, and Japan the Indies. This is what the map looks like today.

Traders from Europe were not welcomed on the land route. So, traders wanted to find an all-water route to the Indies.

People of long ago did not have refrigerators to keep food from going bad. They used spices like pepper, cloves, cinnamon, and nutmeg to cover up the taste of spoiled food. These spices could be found in the Indies.

Kings, queens, and other rich people of long ago loved to dress in fancy silk clothes. Only the people of

These people are gathering spices.

People used spices to cover up the taste of spoiling food.

China knew how to make silk. They did not share their secret of making silk with people of other countries.

Anyone who could find a new route to the Indies would become very rich. Several tries were made to go around Africa. But none had worked. Ships were not very strong, and many ships were lost at sea.

Christopher Columbus spent many years getting ready for his trip.

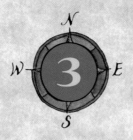

Making Plans

Columbus made a map that showed the world was round. Some people did not believe him.

He believed that most of the world was covered with land. Actually, most of the world is covered with water. Only about one fourth of the world is covered with land. His maps showed that he could reach China by sailing west for a little more than five thousand miles. The world is much bigger than Columbus thought. A ship must sail west about ten thousand miles from Europe to get to China. That is twice as far as Columbus's maps showed. Also, Columbus did not know that North and South America would be in his way.

Columbus drew plans showing the water route to the other side of the world. But he did not have enough money to pay for the ships or to hire men to sail with him.

Columbus asked King John of Portugal to give him money for the trip. King John talked to the men who gave him advice. The men told the king that Columbus's

These men thought Columbus's plans were foolish. They turned their backs on him.

This map shows Columbus's voyage from Italy to Portugal.

plan was foolish. They said that sailing far into the ocean could not be done. So the king did not give Columbus any money.

Columbus knew that he would never get money from King John of Portugal. Then, in 1485, Columbus's wife died. After his wife died, Columbus met Beatriz Enriquez de Arana. They had a son named Ferdinand.

Christopher Columbus decided that he and his son, Diego, would go to Spain. Columbus hoped to show his maps and routes to the king and queen of Spain. Maybe they would give him the money he needed for his trip around the world.

Columbus and Diego took a ship to the city of Palos, Spain. On a high hill above the harbor was a monastery. Columbus asked the monks living there to take care of his son. After hearing about Columbus's plans to sail west, they let Diego live with them. They also helped

Diego stayed with monks while Columbus met with the King and Queen. Some monasteries look like this.

Columbus meet with the king and queen of Spain.

One year later, in 1486, Columbus met Queen Isabella and King Ferdinand. He showed them his maps of the world. He showed them the route he planned to take to the Indies.

Columbus (kneeling) met with Queen Isabella and King Ferdinand of Spain.

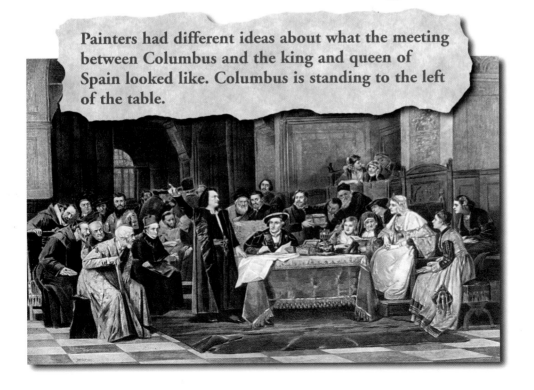

Painters had different ideas about what the meeting between Columbus and the king and queen of Spain looked like. Columbus is standing to the left of the table.

The king and queen listened to his plans. They thought that a new route to the Indies would bring them many riches. They also wanted to spread their religion. If Columbus found new lands, these lands would belong to Spain. New lands would also mean a bigger kingdom.

Isabella and Ferdinand wanted to spread their religion to the new lands.

After six years, they finally gave Columbus the money he needed for his voyage.

They also agreed to several demands that Columbus made if he found the Indies. He wanted to be made a knight and appointed Admiral of the Ocean Sea. He also wanted to be the ruler of any new lands that he found. Finally, Columbus wanted a small share of any new riches he brought back to Spain.

CHRISTOPHER COLUMBUS

Niña

Pinta

Santa María

The Voyage of Discovery

Columbus was given three ships, the *Niña*, the *Pinta*, and the *Santa María*. They became three of the most famous ships in history. The *Niña* and the *Pinta* were small and fast. They were about seventy feet long.

The *Santa María* was the biggest and slowest of the ships. It was about eighty feet long. It was called the flagship. Columbus took charge of the voyage from the *Santa María*. In 1492, ships used sails to make them move. When the wind blew on the sails, the ships moved.

Columbus needed about one hundred men for his ships. Most men were afraid. Some worried about sea

Columbus and his men set sail on August 3, 1492.

monsters. Others feared running out of food and water.

Columbus finally hired eighty-nine sailors for the voyage. The *Niña* had twenty-four men and the *Pinta* had twenty-six men. Columbus and thirty-nine other men sailed on the *Santa María*. Each ship had a pilot to guide it and a doctor to care for the sick. A steward on each ship was in charge of the supplies.

Food for the long trip was packed in barrels. Flour, onions, garlic, olives, figs, and raisins were loaded on the ships. The meat and fish were packed in salt. Salt was used to keep these foods from spoiling. Barrels of wine, oil, and water were loaded on the ships. The ships also carried things like candles, tools, dishes, and firewood.

The ships needed special instruments to keep them on course. One instrument was a quadrant. It helped

Columbus steer the ships by the stars. Another instrument was a compass, which always points north. They also brought a sandglass with them. This was the ship's clock.

The ships had big guns that fired large metal balls. Other weapons on the ships were small guns, crossbows, and swords.

Finally, Columbus brought along a large supply of glass beads, little bells, and other small items. He planned to trade these small items with any people he might meet for gold and spices when he reached the Indies.

Columbus used maps to keep the ships on course. He also used a compass. A sandglass is by Columbus's left hand.

Some of the sailors were angry and frightened because the trip took longer than they thought.

The *Niña*, the *Pinta*, and the *Santa María* left Spain on August 3, 1492. Columbus kept two logs of the trip. A log is the day-to-day record of a ship's voyage. In his own secret log, Columbus wrote how far the ships had really traveled. He did not want the men to know how far they had gone. In the ship's log, he wrote that they had traveled fewer miles.

By late September, the men were very unhappy. Columbus knew the men were plotting to take the ship from him. He kept telling the sailors that land was very near. During the first days of October, some seaweed was spotted. Later some small land birds were seen flying overhead. One morning they saw a branch float past the ships. Now the sailors believed that Columbus was right.

It was early on the morning of October 12, 1492. The sailor who was the lookout for the *Pinta* began shouting, "Land! Land!"

Columbus and his men thought they had finally reached the Indies.

Once land was finally spotted, Columbus and the men took a small boat ashore.

When Columbus and his men finally reached land, they knelt and kissed the ground.

Columbus and his men did not know what they would find in the new land.

The New Land

On October 12, 1492, Columbus and some men took small boats and went ashore. When they got there, they knelt, kissed the sand, and thanked God for the safe trip. Then Columbus planted a flag in the sand, and he set up a cross. He claimed the land for Spain. He called the island San Salvador, which is in the Caribbean Sea.

The people of the land saw the ships. They hurried to shore to see the huge birdlike things. Columbus believed he had reached the Indies so he called the people Indians. These people were probably the Taíno, a tribe of the Arawak people. He gave them beads and other little

The Taíno took the small treasures that Columbus and his men gave them.

things. The Taíno gave Columbus some colorful parrots, balls of cotton thread, and a few pieces of gold.

Columbus was sad. There were no spices and very little gold in San Salvador. Columbus ordered his three ships to sail along the coast. The men were to search for gold and the spices of the Indies.

On December 24, the *Pinta* was miles away from the other two ships. The *Niña* and the *Santa María* were sailing near each other. A young boy was left in charge of the *Santa María*. The boy steered the ship onto some rocks. The rocks tore a hole in the bottom of the ship. Columbus and his men had to leave the sinking ship.

The *Niña* was too small to carry all the sailors from the *Santa María*. Columbus had the men carry the wood from the *Santa María* to shore. The men built a fort and called it Fort Navidad. It was the first Spanish fort in these lands.

Columbus spent ninety-six days searching for gold and spices. Then on January 16, 1493, he began his trip back to Spain. He took the gifts the Taíno had given him. He also took some Taíno men with him. He would use them to show that he had been to the Indies. He left forty men at Fort Navidad. They were to explore the land and search for gold and spices. Columbus promised he would return for the men.

Columbus sailed on the *Niña* for his return trip to Spain. The trip should have been an easy one. The men knew where they were going. But the ships ran into big storms. The ships became separated on

Many honors were given to Columbus for his discovery.

When Columbus returned, he showed King Ferdinand and Queen Isabella what he brought back from his voyage (above). Columbus was also awarded his own coat of arms (right). The castle and lion on the coat of arms stand for royalty. The bottom left section shows islands in the sea. The bottom right section stands for Columbus's family.

February 13, 1493. The two ships had to finish the trip back to Spain alone.

In March 1493, the *Niña* reached Palos, Spain. The *Pinta* stopped at another port first. It reached Palos a few hours after Columbus arrived. Columbus and the crews of the ships were heroes. Many honors were given to Columbus.

The king and queen of Spain were excited about the treasures Columbus had found. Columbus was given seventeen ships, about fifteen hundred men, horses, and supplies for a second voyage across the Great Sea. Christopher Columbus would have more time to explore.

Columbus is known for bringing horses to the new land.

Columbus showed his maps and charts to the king and queen.

Christopher Columbus went on a second voyage.

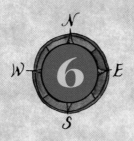

The Changing World

Columbus began his second voyage on September 25, 1493. He sailed to the island of Dominica and to Hispaniola before he reached Fort Navidad. When Columbus reached Fort Navidad, he saw that the fort was burned to the ground. All the men he had left at the fort were dead.

Columbus set up a new settlement. For almost three years, he looked for the treasures of the Indies. Then on June 8, 1496, his ships returned to Spain again with very little gold and no spices. Columbus still believed he had reached the Indies.

On May 30, 1498, Columbus began his third voyage. This time he had only six ships. He had some of the men build another settlement when they reached land. Then Columbus sailed on looking for the treasures of the Indies. Finally after almost two years, he returned to the settlement. He found his men fighting among themselves and with the Taíno.

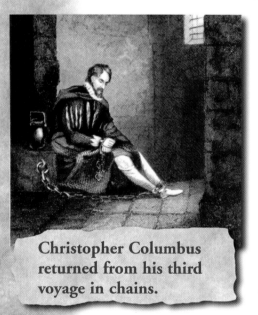

Christopher Columbus returned from his third voyage in chains.

Columbus gave the men land, but this did not make them happy. The men sent letters to the king and queen of Spain. The King sent Francisco de Bobadilla to check on Columbus. After seeing the bad conditions of the settlement, he arrested Columbus and put him in chains. Then he sent Columbus back to Spain. In October 1500, Columbus returned from his third voyage as a prisoner. He was put in jail.

Columbus wrote to the king and queen. He told them what had happened. They believed Columbus and set him free.

On May 11, 1502, Columbus set sail with four ships on his fourth and last voyage across the ocean. This time he spent over two years searching for the treasures of the Indies. But he did not find anything. On November 7, 1504, he returned to Spain.

Christopher Columbus died in Valladolid, Spain, on May 20, 1506. He never knew that he had discovered new lands across the ocean. He died believing he had sailed to the Indies.

Columbus died in May 1506.

Amerigo Vespucci

In 1499, Amerigo Vespucci may have sailed across the ocean. He wrote about the new lands. In 1507, maps were made showing the new lands. The maps had the name of America on the new lands. Today the continents are called North and South America.

The new land was named after Amerigo Vespucci.

What Christopher Columbus Did

Columbus changed many things for the people of the world.

Many sailors started their own adventures. New lands were discovered, and great amounts of gold were found.

The people of Europe learned to like many of the foods that the Taíno and other peoples grew. The explorers brought back corn, peppers, pineapple, squash, tomatoes, peanuts, and beans. People of Europe also learned to use the tobacco that the Indians grew.

Unfortunately, new diseases were brought to Europe from the new land. Many European people died because they did not know much about these diseases.

The people of the new land also had their lives changed forever because of Columbus. The explorers brought new diseases. The medicine men of the Taíno and other tribes did not know anything about these diseases. Sometimes whole tribes died from diseases like measles or smallpox.

Columbus is remembered in many ways. Schools, cities, and rivers are named after him. Colombia, a country in South America, is named in his honor. In the United States, Columbus is remembered with a national holiday. We honor him on Columbus Day, October 12.

In 1541, a map, like the one below, was made. It was the first time the word "America" was used.

Timeline

1451—Christopher Columbus is born in Genoa, Italy.

August 3, 1492—Begins his first voyage.

October 12, 1492—Lands on an island in the Caribbean Sea.

March 1493—Returns from his first voyage.

September 1493—Starts his second voyage.

November 1493—Reaches Hispaniola.

June 8, 1496—Returns from his second voyage.

May 30, 1498—Begins his third voyage.

October 1500—Is arrested and returns home in chains.

May 11, 1502—Sets out for his fourth voyage.

November 7, 1504—Returns from his fourth voyage.

May 20, 1506—Christopher Columbus dies.

Words to Know

astronomy—The study of the stars and planets.

continent—A very large mass of land.

explorer—A person who travels in search of something.

flagship—The ship on which the commander of the fleet sails.

fleet—A group of ships sailing together.

geometry—A kind of math that deals with lines, angles, and shapes.

log—A day-by-day record of a ship's voyage.

lookout—The person who keeps a careful watch for land on a ship.

quadrant—An instrument used to survey or to measure distance.

sandglass—An instrument for measuring time by having sand flow from one section to the another; also called an hourglass.

Learn More About
Christopher Columbus

Books

Chrisp, Peter. *Christopher Columbus: Admiral of the Ocean Sea*. New York: Dorling Kindersley Publishing, Inc., 2001.

Landau, Elaine. *Columbus Day: Celebrating a Famous Explorer*. Berkeley Heights, N.J.: Enslow Publishers, Inc., 2001.

Schaefer, Lola M. *Christopher Columbus*. Minnetonka, Minn.: Capstone Press, Inc., 2002.

Internet Addresses

Christopher Columbus: Explorer

<http://www.enchantedlearning.com/explorers/page/c/columbus.shtml>

Learn more about Christopher Columbus.

Maps and Navigation

<http://tqjunior.thinkquest.org/6169/maps.htm>

As this Web site says, "If you want to be a good sailor, you will need to know about maps and navigation."

Index